# A Love Affair with the Universe

## "Cultivating Synchronicity"

Copyright © 2024 iC7Zi.
All rights reserved.
Published by iC7Zi

# Table of Contents

| | |
|---|---|
| **Preface** <br> • The Importance of Self-Love <br> • Living Without Fear <br> • The Spiritual Law of Decree | 4 |
| **Understanding Self-Love** <br> • Psychological Perspectives on Self-Love <br> • Advaita Vedanta's View of the Self <br> • Barriers to Self-Love <br> • Archetypes and Self-Perception | 12 |
| **The Nature of Self-Sabotage** <br> • Psychological Roots of Self-Sabotage <br> • Overcoming Self-Sabotage <br> • A Path to Inner Freedom | 17 |
| **Fearlessness as a Way of Life** <br> • Fear in the Context of Advaita Vedanta <br> • Techniques to Face and Transcend Fears | 26 |
| **Balancing Letting Go and Wisdom** <br> • Setting Healthy Boundaries <br> • The Dance of Tantra and Mindful Balance | 36 |

**Synchronizing with the Universe** — 43
- Embracing Interconnectedness
- Understanding Synchronicities
- Modern Society and the Disconnect from Our Source
- Embracing Synchronicities
- Attracting Synchronicities
- Differentiating Between Ego and Intuition

**The Quantum Perspective** — 59
- Quantum Principles and Personal Growth
- Connecting Quantum Physics and Spirituality
- Applying Quantum Ideas to Daily Life

**Conclusion** — 66
- Embracing the Deep Sadness and the Void
- The Reality of Death and the Unknown
- Nothingness, God, and the Beyond
- The Named is the Mother
- Faith and Hope as Guiding Stars
- The Journey Forward

**Afterword** — 77

**Affirmations of Inner Truth and Oneness** — 82

**Embracing the Abyss: A Poem** — 84

# Preface

In the quiet depths of our own being lies a profound potential—a wellspring of love, courage, and unity that is often overshadowed by the noise of our fears and doubts.

To embark on the journey of self-love and fearless living is to choose to awaken this potential, to listen to the soft call of our own heart, and to trust that within us lies the power to transform our lives.

This guide is not merely about feeling better but about discovering a deeper truth: that we are whole, connected, and capable of creating a life of genuine purpose.

Here, you are invited to journey beyond superficial goals and societal pressures, stepping into a space where self-love becomes your law, and courage guides your steps.

As you begin this exploration, remember that every insight, every step forward, is a movement toward clarity, joy, and a love that flows effortlessly from within.

This journey is about reclaiming who you are beneath the roles and expectations, about connecting to the universe within and around you, and about realizing that the love you seek is already yours.

## The Importance of Self-Love

Self-love is the cornerstone of a fulfilling life. It is the inner acceptance and appreciation of who we truly are. When we embrace ourselves fully, we unlock the potential for happiness, resilience, and genuine connections with others.

Self-love is not merely a feel-good concept; it's a vital foundation for mental and emotional well-being.

The principle **"Self-love must be the law"** serves as a guiding beacon on this journey. It suggests that before we can extend love outward, we must first cultivate it within ourselves.

By making self-love a personal law, we prioritize our growth and nurture the qualities that allow us to thrive.

## Living Without Fear

Fear often acts as a barrier between us and our fullest expression of life. It can hinder decision-making, stifle creativity, and keep us trapped in cycles of doubt.

The guiding principle **"Do without fear should be the law"** invites us to confront these limitations. It encourages action in the face of uncertainty, promoting courage and the pursuit of our deepest aspirations.

Living without fear doesn't mean the absence of caution but rather embracing life's possibilities without letting fear dictate our choices. It's about trusting ourselves and the journey, even when the path is not entirely clear.

This guide seamlessly blends modern psychological insights with the timeless wisdom of Advaita Vedanta and Taoism.

Advaita Vedanta, a non-dualistic school of Hindu philosophy, reveals the fundamental unity between the individual soul (Atman) and the ultimate reality (Brahman).

Complementing this, Taoism emphasizes living in harmony with the natural flow of existence (Tao), offering profound teachings on balance and inner peace.

Together, these perspectives provide a comprehensive path to understanding oneself and living in alignment with the universe.

Psychology offers tools to understand the mind and behavior, helping us identify patterns that hinder self-love and courage. Advaita Vedanta provides a spiritual framework that transcends the ego and connects us to a greater whole.

The mind should be seen as a tool, not the master; when the mind assumes control, it can become a source of turmoil. Your mind is not inherently your friend—it must be trained and guided to become the best tool in your toolkit.

By integrating these perspectives, we aim to create a holistic approach that addresses both the psychological and spiritual dimensions of self-growth. This fusion allows for a deeper exploration of the Self, bridging the gap between mind and spirit.

The intention of this guide is to lead you on a transformative journey toward embracing self-love and living fearlessly. Through understanding and practice, you will learn to:

- Recognize and overcome barriers to self-love.
- Navigate life with courage and authenticity.
- Differentiate between the ego's voice and true intuition.
- Connect deeply with the universe and experience meaningful synchronicities.
- Apply insights from quantum physics to understand the interconnectedness of all things.

By the end of this journey, you'll have the tools and insights to cultivate a loving relationship with yourself and the universe around you.

As the complexities fall away, what remains is a life of simplicity, purpose, joy, and the quiet truth of deep connection.

## The Spiritual Law of Decree

There is a profound power in the Law of Decree, a principle that aligns the might of the universe behind a singular, conscious statement of intent.

Unlike affirmations or prayers, which are often repeated to reinforce belief and energy, a decree is made once—with unwavering clarity and certainty.

It is a direct call to the universe, a statement imbued with the authority of your deepest Self, summoning the forces of creation to align with your will.

When we initiate the Law of Decree, we call forth the essence of the All—the Absolute Reality, the One beyond form and thought.

This practice is an invocation of our oneness with the universal consciousness, drawing upon the boundless potential that exists within and around us.

Decrees serve as a reminder of our innate connection to the creative source of life, reinforcing our role as co-creators of our reality.

**Examples of Generalized Decrees:**

- "By the will of the All, under the grace of the Absolute, I decree that every limiting belief, thought pattern, and attachment within me is now transformed and released. So it is."

- "In the name of the One True Source, under the light of truth, I decree that all past vows and bonds which no longer serve my highest path are now dissolved and set free. Let it be done."

- "By divine will, aligned with the Beyond, I call forth a stream of pure light to envelop my being and guide me with unconditional love. It is so."

A decree is not simply a request or wish; it is an assertion of trust and power—a declaration that you stand united with the infinite, drawing its boundless energy into your present moment.

Through this practice, we claim our rightful place in the cosmic dance, embracing the deep truth that we are, indeed, one with the universe and capable of shaping our lives with purpose and unwavering resolve.

The Law of Decree works best when you understand the dance between the energies of one and two, and how they interplay and reverse.

In numerology, the number **1** embodies masculine energy—assertive, initiating, and focused. It represents action, leadership, and determination.

On the other hand, the number **2** symbolizes feminine energy—intuitive, nurturing, and harmonious. It embodies balance, receptivity, and the subtle power of connection.

Understanding this balance is crucial: **1** drives forward with purpose, while **2** listens and aligns with deeper wisdom. The dance between these energies reflects the dynamic flow of life itself, where assertiveness and intuition, action and reflection, must coexist.

First, cultivate self-love (the foundation of **1**), then extend that love outward, nurturing and expanding it (the essence of **2**). This harmonious interaction lays the groundwork for using the Law of Decree effectively.

By mastering the balance between the masculine and feminine, the active and receptive, and understanding when to reverse their order, you'll be better equipped to transform your inner world and, by extension, your outer reality.

There are times when the natural sequence is **1** followed by **2**—acting assertively and then tempering it with intuition.

However, in other moments, **2** leads with intuition and receptivity, followed by **1** to take decisive, informed action. Knowing when to play **1 and 2** or **2 and 1** is key to mastering this balance.

Always remember, behind every **1** lies the zero, and behind every **2** lies the zero—the void, the nothingness, the unknown.

This is the Absolute Reality, the true doer, the silent force from which all creation flows.

Understand this deeply. Feel it as a pulse beneath existence, observe its quiet power. As Lao Tzu said,

> The tao that can be told
> is not the eternal Tao
> The name that can be named
> is not the eternal Name.
>
> The unnamable is the eternally real.
> Naming is the origin
> of all particular things.
>
> Free from desire, you realize the mystery.
> Caught in desire, you see only the manifestations.
>
> Yet mystery and manifestations
> arise from the same source.
> This source is called darkness.
>
> Darkness within darkness.
> The gateway to all understanding.

Let this eternal space guide you, for it holds the essence of all energy and the mysteries that move through every action and intention.

Let your breath flow; do not hold it. Give your full attention to the gentle rise and fall. Take deep, nourishing breaths.

Allow the energy to move within you, carried by each breath. Let it flow freely, unrestrained, and let it awaken the quiet power within.

The following chapters will guide you through practices and insights to help you execute the Law of Decree with greater awareness and impact.

These chapters are simple, yet within their simplicity lies the paradox of complexity and the path beyond duality.

# Chapter 1:

# Understanding Self-Love

## Psychological Perspectives on Self-Love

Self-love, in psychological terms, is the regard for one's own well-being and happiness. It involves nurturing oneself with respect, compassion, and acceptance.

Psychologists view self-love as a vital component of mental health, influencing how we perceive ourselves and interact with the world. It encompasses self-esteem, self-worth, and self-compassion.

From this perspective, self-love is not narcissism or selfishness; rather, it's about recognizing one's inherent value. It involves:

- **Self-Acceptance:** Embracing all facets of oneself—strengths and weaknesses alike.

- **Self-Care:** Prioritizing one's physical, emotional, and mental needs.

- **Self-Respect:** Setting boundaries and honoring personal values.

## Advaita Vedanta's View of the Self

Advaita Vedanta offers a profound spiritual understanding of the self. It teaches that the true Self (Atman) is not separate from the ultimate reality (Brahman). In essence, every individual soul is a reflection of the universal consciousness.

Key concepts include:

- **Non-Duality:** There is no separation between the self and the universe; all is one.

- **Illusion of the Ego:** The ego creates a false sense of individuality, leading to suffering.

- **Self-Realization:** Understanding one's true nature brings liberation (moksha).

In this philosophy, self-love transcends the personal ego and aligns with universal love. It's about recognizing that by loving oneself, one is also loving the entirety of existence.

## Barriers to Self-Love

From a young age, society inundates us with messages about who we should be. Cultural norms, media portrayals, and familial expectations can shape our self-perception negatively.

Common societal barriers include:

- **Idealized Standards:** Unrealistic beauty and success ideals can lead to feelings of inadequacy.

- **Comparison Culture:** Social media fosters constant comparisons, undermining self-worth.

- **Conformity Pressures:** Deviating from societal norms may result in judgment or rejection.

These external pressures can distance us from our authentic selves, making self-love challenging.

Over time, negative experiences and criticisms can become internalized, forming limiting beliefs about ourselves.

Examples include:

- **"I'm not good enough."**

- **"I don't deserve happiness."**

- **"Failure defines me."**

These beliefs act as mental scripts, influencing our thoughts and behaviors. They create a cycle of self-doubt and self-criticism, obstructing the path to self-love.

## Archetypes and Self-Perception

Archetypes are universal symbols and patterns of behavior residing in the collective unconscious, as proposed by psychologist Carl Jung. Certain archetypes can impede self-love by reinforcing negative self-images.

Key hindering archetypes:

- **The Perfectionist:** Strives for flawlessness, leading to constant dissatisfaction.

- **The People-Pleaser:** Prioritizes others' needs over personal well-being.

- **The Victim:** Feels powerless, blaming external factors for personal unhappiness.

- **The Critic:** Harbors an inner voice that constantly judges and devalues self-worth.

Understanding how these archetypes play out can help in recognizing and overcoming them.

- **The Perfectionist** may avoid taking risks unless success is guaranteed, limiting growth opportunities.

- **The People-Pleaser** might agree to tasks they dislike, causing stress and resentment.

- **The Victim** may resist change, feeling stuck in unfavorable situations.

- **The Critic** can lead to harsh self-talk, impacting confidence and decision-making.

By identifying these patterns, we can begin to challenge and transform them, clearing the way for genuine self-love.

# Chapter 2:

# The Nature of Self-Sabotage

Self-sabotage refers to behaviors and thought patterns that undermine our own success and well-being.

It's an internal conflict where conscious desires are thwarted by subconscious motives, leading to actions that hinder progress toward personal goals.

Common self-sabotaging behaviors include:

- **Procrastination:** Delaying tasks to avoid discomfort, fear of failure, or responsibility.

- **Negative Self-Talk:** Engaging in internal dialogues that are critical and discouraging.

- **Avoidance:** Steering clear of situations or opportunities that could lead to growth due to fear of change.

- **Overindulgence:** Excessive behaviors (e.g., overeating, substance abuse) used as coping mechanisms.

Thought patterns often involve:

- **All-or-Nothing Thinking:** Viewing situations in black-and-white terms without acknowledging nuances.

- **Catastrophizing:** Expecting the worst possible outcome, magnifying problems beyond their actual impact.

- **Self-Defeating Beliefs:** Holding onto convictions like "I'm not good enough" or "I don't deserve success."

Recognizing these patterns is crucial. Awareness is the first step toward interrupting the cycle of self-sabotage.

## Psychological Roots of Self-Sabotage

- **Fear of Failure:** The prospect of failing can be so daunting that it prevents us from taking action. Past experiences of failure may contribute to anxiety about repeating mistakes, leading to paralysis or avoidance.

- **Fear of Success:** Success can bring increased expectations, visibility, and pressure. The unfamiliar territory of success may cause discomfort, prompting behaviors that sabotage progress to return to a familiar (albeit unsatisfying) status quo.

These fears can create internal conflicts where the desire for achievement is counteracted by the comfort of familiarity and safety.

- **Internalized Criticism:** Negative feedback from influential figures during formative years can become internalized, leading to persistent self-doubt.

- **Traumatic Experiences:** Past trauma can distort self-perception, making individuals feel unworthy or incapable of success.

- **Comparisons:** Constantly measuring oneself against others can erode self-esteem, especially when focusing on perceived shortcomings.

Low self-worth fuels self-sabotage by reinforcing the belief that one doesn't deserve happiness or success, thus manifesting behaviors that align with that belief.

## Overcoming Self-Sabotage

Start by becoming more aware of your thoughts, emotions, and behaviors. This self-awareness is foundational for lasting change. Mindfulness practices, such as meditation or mindful breathing, help attune you to the present, where awareness begins.

Journaling can be a powerful tool—writing down your thoughts and behaviors over time can reveal patterns that might otherwise go unnoticed.

Regular reflection, where you assess your choices and actions, allows you to uncover underlying motivations, aligning your actions with your true Self.

**Reframing Negative Thought Patterns**

Challenging negative patterns requires a gentle, patient approach. Begin by identifying limiting beliefs that may be holding you back. Cognitive restructuring techniques can help you replace irrational beliefs with constructive, positive alternatives.

Use <u>affirmations</u> to reinforce self-belief, and gather evidence of past successes to remind yourself of your resilience.

Neuroplasticity, the brain's ability to rewire and adapt, means that with time and persistence, you can form new, empowering thought patterns.

Remember, transformation takes time, but every small step forward is meaningful progress.

**Setting Realistic Goals**

Setting realistic goals is essential for avoiding overwhelm and staying motivated. Break larger objectives into smaller, manageable steps. This makes your goals feel achievable, keeping you on track toward progress.

Aim for SMART goals—Specific, Measurable, Achievable, Relevant, and Time-bound—so you stay focused and clear about your intentions.

Celebrate each milestone, no matter how small; recognizing achievements, even minor ones, fuels motivation and creates a positive reinforcement cycle.

## Developing Healthy Coping Mechanisms

Life is filled with challenges, and developing healthy coping mechanisms helps manage the ups and downs effectively. Stress management techniques like deep breathing, yoga, or any form of movement can ground you and create calm.

Engage in creative outlets such as art, music, or writing to express and process emotions. Lean on support systems, whether that's family, friends, or professionals who can offer guidance and understanding. There's no shame in reaching out for support.

Change is often a gradual process, and it's okay to seek help when you need it—growth is not a solo journey.

## Embracing Self-Compassion

Treat yourself with kindness and patience, recognizing that mistakes are part of the human experience. Self-compassion allows you to let go of perfectionism, giving yourself the freedom to learn and grow.

When you make a misstep, approach it as an opportunity rather than a failure. Neuroplasticity shows us that with time, self-compassion itself can become a default response, nurturing a supportive inner environment that enhances resilience.

## Aligning Actions with Core Values

Identify what matters most to you, your core values, and let these be the compass for your decisions. Purposeful living arises from aligning your daily actions with these values, ensuring that even small steps forward reinforce long-term goals.

Consistency is key, but so is flexibility—allow yourself to adapt as your values and goals evolve. Each action rooted in your core values strengthens your commitment to a life of meaning and fulfillment.

## Transformation Takes Time

The journey of self-love, self-compassion, and change takes time and patience. Trust in the process of neuroplasticity—your brain's capacity to reshape itself in response to new habits and beliefs.

Every small, positive step is reshaping your inner world and building a lasting foundation for well-being.

Be kind to yourself along the way, celebrate your progress, and know that meaningful transformation is not only possible but already underway as you commit to each moment of growth.

These steps will help dismantle self-sabotage and foster a healthier, more empowering relationship with yourself.

The journey of self-awareness, goal-setting, and self-compassion may seem like an endless pursuit, leading some to wonder,

"Why must I go through all of this just to live?"

The truth is, even as we achieve these milestones, an unnameable void may remain—a silent presence within us that no success or accomplishment can fill.

This void, however, is not something to fear but to embrace. It is from this space that true compassion arises, an acceptance of our shared humanity and a deep, abiding love for both ourselves and others.

Life becomes a dance of presence and surrender, where we engage fully yet release attachment to outcomes.

In Tantra, this is akin to the practice of "surrendering into the moment," merging with the flow of life to discover profound joy and love beyond the ego self.

Through this lens, each experience, whether joyous or painful, invites us to see life with deeper reverence, cultivating a love that transcends individual desires and connects us to the essence of existence itself.

# A Path to Inner Freedom

Advaita Vedanta, the non-dual philosophy rooted in the ancient Upanishads, provides profound insight into the nature of self-sabotage and transformation.

According to this tradition, at the core of our being, we are not separate individuals struggling through a fractured existence, but rather, we are the **Atman**—the true Self, which is one with **Brahman**, the infinite reality.

The perception of separation, where we see ourselves as isolated and lacking, is called **Maya**, the veil of illusion.

Self-sabotage, seen through this lens, is not just a set of behaviors or beliefs to overcome; it is the natural result of identifying with the ego-self ('Ahamkara'), which clings to limited perceptions and fears. The Upanishads remind us:

> "Brahman is the whole; Atman is the whole; from wholeness comes wholeness; take wholeness from wholeness, and wholeness remains."
>
> — Isa Upanishad

This means that our essence is already complete, untouched by the patterns of self-sabotage and doubt.

Self-sabotaging behaviors arise when we forget our true nature and attach ourselves to fleeting experiences and external validations. The Mundaka Upanishad guides us with:

> "Know the Self to be pure and immortal. Know the Self to be beyond the body, beyond the senses, beyond the mind. It is everywhere, always still, eternal."

This knowledge shifts the journey from one of self-improvement to self-realization. We do not need to fix ourselves because we are already whole; we only need to recognize this.

Awareness becomes a path back to unity. The practice of **Neti, Neti** ("not this, not this") teaches us to disidentify from the mental constructs and limiting beliefs that fuel self-sabotage.

We can witness the fear of failure, the internalized criticism, and the comparisons, but with the understanding that these are not who we truly are. The Katha Upanishad says,

> "When all desires that dwell in the heart fall away, then the mortal becomes immortal and attains Brahman in this very life."

To move beyond self-sabotage is to release desires rooted in ego and align with the quiet essence of our being.

In practical terms, embracing Advaita means practicing self-inquiry, asking, "**Who am I?**" repeatedly, not to seek a thought-based answer but to dissolve into the awareness behind the question. We will go into more detail on this question in a later chapter.

Self-sabotage loses power when one realizes that the thinker of self-defeating thoughts is itself an illusion.

This shift to non-dual awareness transforms how we view obstacles. Life's challenges and self-sabotaging tendencies are not failures; they are opportunities for recognizing and remembering our true nature.

We begin to act not from a place of lack or fear but from a deep, unshakeable awareness that we are already complete. Embracing this understanding brings about a profound inner freedom, where every action is aligned with the wholeness of existence itself.

As the Mandukya Upanishad reveals,

> "The Self is the source of all; it is beyond all duality, beyond all division."

Through the lens of Advaita Vedanta, overcoming self-sabotage becomes not just a pursuit of personal betterment, but a path to realizing our oneness with the divine essence of life.

This realization dissolves the need for external validation and allows us to move through life with peace, presence, and boundless love.

# Chapter 3:

# Fearlessness as a Way of Life

Fear is a fundamental human emotion, an innate response designed to protect us from danger. It triggers the "fight or flight" reaction, preparing the body to respond to threats.

Psychologically, fear arises from the perception of risk or harm, whether physical, emotional, or psychological.

Key aspects include:

- **Evolutionary Roots:** Fear has been essential for survival, alerting us to dangers in our environment.

- **Learned Responses:** Past experiences can condition us to fear certain stimuli, even when they're no longer threatening.

- **Cognitive Processes:** Our thoughts and interpretations play a significant role in how we experience fear.

Common psychological triggers of fear are:

- **Uncertainty:** The unknown can provoke anxiety about potential negative outcomes.

- **Loss of Control:** Feeling powerless can intensify fear responses.

- **Ego Threats:** Challenges to our self-image or identity can elicit fear, leading to defensive behaviors.

Understanding these roots helps us recognize that while fear is natural, it can sometimes be disproportionate or misplaced, hindering personal growth.

## Fear in the Context of Advaita Vedanta

In Advaita Vedanta, fear is seen not as a fixed reality but as a shadow cast by ignorance (Avidya) about our true nature.

The philosophy teaches that our essence—the Self or Atman—is not a fleeting form, but an eternal spark, inseparable from the vast, unchanging consciousness known as Brahman. This understanding dissolves the illusion of separateness, which is at the heart of fear.

Fear emerges only when we identify with the ego and the physical body, mistaking ourselves for vulnerable, isolated beings subject to loss, suffering, and death.

Advaita Vedanta speaks to the **illusion of separation**, or the belief that we exist independently from the rest of existence. This illusion reinforces a false sense of identity tied to the material world, what Vedanta calls **Maya**.

Maya is the powerful illusion that convinces us that this world of forms and changes is the only reality, distracting us from the true Self that lies beneath. "Just as a snake appears in a rope in the dark," Shankara wrote, "so the world appears in Brahman due to ignorance."

In other words, the fears we feel and the attachments we hold are merely perceptions, rooted in misidentification with temporary forms and experiences.

**The Mind and Its Illusions**

The mind itself, though a powerful tool for navigating the world, is also a source of illusion. It divides, categorizes, and analyzes, creating a perception of duality where there is none.

Often decisive and quick to judge, the mind attaches labels and meaning to everything, building a complex world of beliefs and dogmas that can keep us bound in limitation.

In this way, the mind is both a guide and a trap—it can illuminate or obscure our path. But it is essential to recognize that **the mind is not the ultimate reality**.

Beyond the mind lies the expansive awareness of the Self, unconditioned and free from the dualities that the mind imposes.

To realize this truth is to understand that the mind can never fully grasp the totality of existence. As the Katha Upanishad states,

> "The Self is beyond thought and the senses, beyond the grasp of the mind."

Awareness of the mind's limitations brings us closer to that which lies beyond it, to a state of deep presence, and to the discovery that our thoughts and beliefs are passing clouds against the clear sky of consciousness.

## The Trap of Dogmatic Religion

Dogma in religion, whether from the East or West, often diverts true seekers from genuine spiritual discovery.

Organized belief systems frequently mistake external rituals and doctrines for spiritual truths, but as mystics across traditions have recognized, **true religion transcends the forms and boundaries of any specific practice or doctrine**.

Those who cling too tightly to these dogmas, interpreting them literally and without introspection, often know the least about the true essence of religion.

Religions are meant to point to something beyond the structures they create. Yet, when they are seen as the ultimate truth rather than as a gateway to it, they become barriers rather than pathways to self-realization.

It is essential for each individual to look beyond dogmatic teachings and embrace the spiritual core that religions attempt to convey—the unity and interconnectedness of all existence.

## The Dance of Shiva and Shakti

To move beyond fear and into a deeper understanding of existence, we must cultivate an awareness of our interconnectedness with the universe, an understanding that goes beyond intellectual acknowledgment to become a lived reality.

In Tantric teachings, Shiva represents pure consciousness, the stillness beyond all form, while Shakti is the creative energy that manifests the cosmos.

Their union symbolizes the interconnectedness of all that is—consciousness and energy, stillness and movement, void and form.

Engaging in the "affair" of Shiva and Shakti means embodying the awareness of both dimensions. It involves recognizing that while we are expressions of pure consciousness, we are also interconnected with the vibrant play of life.

This understanding fosters compassion, as we see that each person, each experience, and each moment is a manifestation of the divine interplay of these energies.

To love oneself and others deeply, to embrace life with reverence and understanding, is to live in harmony with this cosmic dance.

In cultivating this awareness, we begin to see that life, with all its complexities and dualities, is a continuous expression of unity. The fear of separation, death, or loss begins to dissolve, and in its place arises a profound love for all that exists. As Rumi once wrote,

> "You are not a drop in the ocean; you are the entire ocean in a drop."

When we truly understand this, fear fades, leaving us in silence—a silence that speaks of love, unity, and the infinite nature of our true Self.

## Techniques to Face and Transcend Fears

Building courage is not about eliminating fear but learning to face and transcend it in ways that expand our capacity to live fully.

Techniques to confront fear often begin with cultivating self-awareness and presence, challenging negative thought patterns, and finding gentle ways to approach what scares us.

**Mindfulness and Self-Awareness**

One of the first steps in overcoming fear is to become more aware of it without judgment. By observing your reactions mindfully, you can identify the thoughts, situations, or experiences that trigger fear.

Once you understand what lies beneath, fears become more approachable, allowing you to respond rather than react.

**Challenging and Reframing Negative Thoughts**

Our minds often exaggerate threats, creating worst-case scenarios. By questioning the validity of these fearful thoughts, we can reframe them into more balanced perspectives.

Simple affirmations—such as reminding ourselves of our strengths—can replace fear-driven beliefs with empowering statements, reinforcing a positive mindset.

**Facing Fears Gradually**

One effective way to weaken the grip of fear is by gradually exposing yourself to what scares you, a practice often called "exposure therapy."

Starting with small steps, you begin to confront fears in manageable doses. Over time, this reduces their impact, building resilience and helping you to reclaim your power over them.

**Breathing and Relaxation Techniques**

To manage the physical symptoms of fear, deep breathing and relaxation techniques can be incredibly helpful. Slow, mindful breathing activates the body's calming response, reducing tension.

## Visualization

Positive visualization is a powerful tool to transform fear into confidence. Imagine yourself successfully facing situations that normally induce fear, allowing yourself to feel the sense of accomplishment.

Additionally, creating a mental "safe space" can offer a calming retreat for the mind during moments of overwhelm.

To create this sanctuary within, close your eyes and take deep, mindful breaths. Imagine a space that feels sacred and peaceful to you—a serene forest, a quiet room filled with warm light, or an open field under a starlit sky.

Immerse yourself fully in this mental haven, focusing on every detail.

As you settle into this space, practice non-duality by recognizing that all boundaries dissolve in the presence of the true Self, the Atman, which is one with Brahman, the ultimate reality.

Allow your safe space to become a reflection of this oneness, feeling the unity between yourself and the surroundings. Sit in stillness and observe your thoughts as passing waves on the ocean of consciousness—temporary and separate from your true, unchanging essence.

Return to this space regularly to reconnect with the sense of wholeness and boundless peace that lies at the heart of your being.

## Self-Compassion

Recognize fear as a natural part of being human, and treat yourself kindly when you feel vulnerable. Accept your emotions without criticism, and approach your journey with patience.

Self-compassion reinforces resilience, allowing you to approach challenges as opportunities for growth rather than sources of defeat.

## Spiritual Connection

Practices such as meditation or self-inquiry, especially in the Advaita Vedanta tradition, help deepen your connection to the Self beyond the ego.

By contemplating the question "Who am I?" and discovering the timeless Self beyond thoughts and fears, you can transcend the limitations of the mind and connect to an unshakable source of peace.

In the Advaita Vedanta tradition, the question "Who am I?" is more than a philosophical inquiry; it's a powerful, transformative practice that guides us beyond the illusions of the ego.

This practice, known as **self-inquiry (Atma Vichara)**, invites us to turn our attention inward, seeking the truth of our identity not in what we have, what we do, or even what we think, but in the awareness that perceives all these experiences.

Typically, our sense of self is tied to transient elements: our name, body, beliefs, achievements, and social roles. However, these identifiers are impermanent and ever-changing.

If we define ourselves by what is temporary, our sense of self will always be fragile, vulnerable to change, and at the mercy of external events.

The ego clings to these surface-level identities, but it does so out of fear—fear of death, fear of insignificance, fear of the unknown.

When we ask "Who am I?" in meditation or contemplation, we are not seeking an answer in words but an experiential awareness. As you sit with the question, layers of identity begin to fall away, like shedding masks.

You realize, "I am not my body, as my body changes; I am not my thoughts, as they are fleeting; I am not my emotions, as they come and go." With each realization, you move closer to the essence that remains when all these layers are removed.

Through self-inquiry, what emerges is the realization that the true Self—the Atman—is not bound by the limitations of the mind or the body. This Self is pure consciousness, the unchanging witness to all thoughts, experiences, and sensations.

It is neither born nor dies, untouched by fears or desires. This awareness of the Self, which is beyond all dualities, offers a sense of peace and freedom that is unshakable, as it is not dependent on external circumstances.

Ramana Maharshi, a modern sage of Advaita Vedanta, taught that by seeking the source of the "I" thought, we uncover a silent, ever-present awareness—a deeper Self that exists beyond our usual identification with the ego.

He explained, "The 'I' thought will die if you take refuge in its source." In other words, when we look inward and question the origin of our sense of "I," the ego begins to dissolve.

What remains is a pure presence, an awareness that feels both deeply personal and universally connected, beyond any individual identity or thought.

The mind is an excellent servant but a poor master. It creates endless stories, judgments, and fears, binding us to the ego's limitations. However, **the mind is not the ultimate reality**; it's simply a tool.

Self-inquiry reveals that while thoughts arise in the mind, they are like waves on the surface of the ocean. Beneath the mind's fluctuations lies a vast, still awareness—the true Self.

Realizing that the mind is only a construct allows us to experience life from a place of presence and peace, untouched by the ego's dramas.

As you explore the question "Who am I?" the ego loses its grip, and a more profound understanding of existence emerges. You begin to see yourself as part of an interconnected whole, not as a separate, isolated individual.

This realization cultivates a deep compassion, both for oneself and others, as you recognize that we are all expressions of the same universal consciousness.

This is where the symbolic union of **Shiva and Shakti**—consciousness and energy, stillness and movement—comes alive. Life becomes a dance of unity, a play of forms, all arising from and returning to the same source.

Ultimately, the question "Who am I?" is not meant to yield an answer but to dissolve the questioner, revealing a state of being that is boundless, timeless, and free. It is in this realization that true peace, wisdom, and love are found.

When we live with courage, fear no longer confines us; it propels us toward our truest, fullest expression. By consciously engaging in these practices, we turn fear into a tool for growth.

Living "without fear" becomes an affirmation of life itself—a transformative process that allows us to expand, explore, and live with joy, authenticity, and profound freedom.

# Chapter 4:

# Balancing Letting Go and Wisdom

Life offers us peak experiences—moments of profound joy, insight, and connection that leave lasting impressions on our hearts and minds.

These experiences, whether as vast as watching a sunset or as intimate as a meaningful conversation, shape our understanding of ourselves and the world.

To fully appreciate these moments, it's essential to be present, immersing ourselves without judgment or distraction.

In this openness, we connect deeply, notice life's subtleties, and feel the joy of pure experience.

Openness is the key to embracing life's richness. By letting go of preconceptions, we allow ourselves to learn, grow, and heal.

New ideas can broaden our horizons, past wounds can find release, and inspiration can flow freely. In this way, openness becomes not just a state of mind but a gateway to personal transformation.

Yet, true openness requires discernment. While being open fosters growth, blind acceptance can lead to naivety. Openness should be paired with wisdom to avoid gullibility. Where openness encourages exploration, discernment provides caution.

For example, critical thinking allows us to examine information and validate its sources, while mindfulness keeps us aware of our biases. This balance between openness and skepticism lets us remain receptive to new experiences without losing ourselves to them.

Avoiding naivety requires recognizing common pitfalls. Overidealizing people or situations can cloud judgment. The fear of missing out (FOMO) often pushes us to act impulsively, while the desire for quick fixes may lead us to accept shallow solutions.

By understanding these tendencies, we cultivate an approach that honors both openness and wisdom, protecting ourselves from harm while staying curious and engaged.

Mindfulness brings conscious awareness to the present moment. By practicing mindfulness, we develop emotional resilience and clarity, helping us manage reactions and perceive situations with greater accuracy.

Meanwhile, critical thinking encourages us to analyze and question information, allowing us to make informed decisions and avoid being misled.

Together, mindfulness and critical thinking create a powerful toolkit for navigating life's complexities with clarity and insight.

Mindfulness involves pausing, observing, and grounding ourselves in the here and now. Critical thinking complements this by encouraging us to question our assumptions, analyze information, and reflect on consequences.

Integrating these practices strengthens our capacity for balanced, wise living.

The true currency of life is your attention; where your attention goes, growth follows—whether it leads to abundance or destruction depends on your intention.

Attention is the focused energy you direct toward an object or thought, while intention is the purpose or goal behind that focus.

Take a moment to reflect: who or what is harnessing your attention, and with what motive? This awareness can only be cultivated through stillness, being silent in your breath.

When you anchor yourself in the present moment, you strengthen your intuitive power and evolve on a soul level.

If you sense that you are being used or drained, pause and take a conscious breath; this act will fortify your aura, the spiritual field of energy that surrounds and protects you.

In the spiritual sense, the aura reflects your inner state, embodying your emotions, thoughts, and intentions.

By focusing your attention inward, using the breath as your anchor, and setting the intention of peace, you begin to see through the distractions around you.

You will recognize the external circus—a grand distraction meant to divert attention from deeper truths.

In ancient times, it was the Roman colosseum, where entertainment concealed the realities of life. Today, it is like a football match that captivates the masses, keeping hidden the underlying issues that go unnoticed.

This game exploits the shadow side of human nature: aggression, jealousy, and fear. Yet, these same energies can be transmuted into their higher forms—courage, admiration, and love.

Consider what surrounds these spectacles: the ads, the food, the drinks they promote. Are these offerings enhancing your well-being and strengthening your immune system, or are they depleting it?

The intention is not to avoid the play of life but to engage with it consciously—enjoying when and how you choose, rather than being harnessed by large corporations who treat the masses like cattle on a farm.

True enjoyment comes from awareness and choice, not from being driven by external forces that profit from your unexamined participation.

Remember, be unapologetically selfish in your spiritual journey. This does not mean self-serving in the material sense, but placing your spiritual growth as your highest priority.

Whatever is meant for you will align with this path.

Humans embody both devils and angels; one will lead you astray with ego, and the other with naive innocence.

Your task is to balance these energies, seeing people, situations, and life as they are—free from projections of fear or excessive goodwill.

Cultivate this understanding by sitting with yourself, embracing the void and the nothingness within. At first, this practice may seem daunting, as the subconscious mind releases stored traumas in unexpected ways.

Yet, this is part of the process. Keep moving forward, and you will find doors opening in miraculous and unforeseen ways.

Support will come to you, feeling like a divine gift, guiding you further on your journey of self-discovery and spiritual ascension.

## Setting Healthy Boundaries

Healthy boundaries are essential to balancing openness and self-protection. Boundaries define what is acceptable in interactions, safeguarding our physical, emotional, and mental well-being.

Setting boundaries prevents burnout, fosters respect, and strengthens self-empowerment. They allow us to be open without compromising our integrity or energy.

Establishing boundaries begins with self-awareness. Knowing what we value and recognizing our limits helps us set boundaries that align with our needs.

Effective communication is key; expressing boundaries clearly and assertively ensures mutual respect in relationships. Consistency reinforces boundaries over time, while flexibility allows them to adapt to changing circumstances.

Healthy boundaries create a safe space for exploration. They allow us to selectively share and engage, using discernment to determine when openness is appropriate.

By setting limits, we honor our intuition and protect our well-being, cultivating a balanced life where openness and self-respect coexist.

As we learn to balance letting go with discernment, we become more present, authentic, and resilient. Embracing peak experiences enriches our lives, while discernment ensures we navigate them wisely.

This delicate equilibrium allows us to live fully and engage deeply, fostering a life of purpose, joy, and profound connection with ourselves and the world around us.

In the words of Lao Tzu:

"Knowing others is intelligence; knowing yourself is true wisdom."

Wisdom and self-awareness go hand in hand, allowing us to explore life with openness, yet guided by the wisdom of our own inner compass.

## The Dance of Tantra and Mindful Balance

In your journey toward embracing life's peak experiences, remember that true transformation lies in balancing flow and steadiness. The essence of Tantra is to fully experience life, to engage with its deepest joys and intensities.

Yet, to do so wisely, one must anchor in mindfulness. This may seem like a paradox at first, but true wisdom often hides in such paradoxes, guiding us beyond the illusions of duality.

**Tantra with mindfulness** is the key to navigating life's waves. It teaches us to surrender to the divine energy of Shakti—the creative force that embodies spontaneity, passion, and flow.

When you give yourself to Shakti, you allow yourself to be moved by grace, embracing the fullness of every moment, feeling life's pulse in every fiber of your being. But with this flow comes the need for discernment, the need to anchor.

Like Shiva, the eternal observer and the unmoving center, mindfulness becomes your anchor. Shiva symbolizes pure consciousness, the unchanging awareness that holds space for Shakti's dance.

To live in balance means knowing when to surrender to life's currents and when to stand firm in stillness. This interplay of movement and rest, of passion and peace, is the heart of true wisdom.

Esoteric teachings remind us that Shakti without Shiva becomes chaotic energy, while Shiva without Shakti is lifeless stillness. Together, they form a harmonious whole, embodying the dance of existence itself.

In the same way, Tantra practiced with mindfulness allows you to immerse in the beauty of peak experiences while staying anchored in your true Self.

Recognize when to flow with life's grace and when to hold your ground in presence. This balance, cultivated through practice, enables you to transcend surface living and touch the essence of existence.

It empowers you to harness the energy of life's paradoxes—to move beyond mere duality into a state where love, joy, and peace are not fleeting, but enduring.

Embrace this dance, and you will find that even amidst the most profound experiences, you remain rooted in the quiet, unshakeable center of your being.

This is where true transformation unfolds—where you become both the dancer and the stillness, the wave and the ocean, Shakti and Shiva, in perfect harmony.

# Chapter 5:

# Synchronizing with the Universe

The universe is more than a vast collection of stars, galaxies, and cosmic events; it is a living web of intelligence, and we are not separate from it. If we, as humans, possess intelligence, can we not imagine that the universe itself is intelligent too?

Nature, with its intricate patterns and rhythms, holds a wisdom beyond our understanding. Every river flowing, every leaf unfurling, every star shining—these are expressions of an intelligence that pulses through all of existence.

We are woven into this fabric, not as mere observers but as participants in a profound and intimate dance.

Yet, as humans, we often approach the unknown with labels and categories. If something defies our comprehension, we name it, put it in a box, and assure ourselves we have understood it. But life is far more mysterious than our minds can contain.

To truly know life, we must go beyond labels, beyond definitions, and embrace it as a living mystery. We must have the courage to experience life personally, directly, without trying to capture it with words.

Personal experiences are our teachers, offering us glimpses of life's depth. They give us strength, resilience, and the humility to accept what cannot be understood.

These moments remind us to "wink at the universe," to enter into a playful, trusting relationship with existence itself. Rumi said,

> "Do not be satisfied with the stories that come before you. Unfold your own myth."

Always trust your innate powers and listen to your inner voice— not the voice clouded by guilt, fear, or judgment, but the voice that empowers you, drives your growth, and fuels your expansion.

Don't take things at face value; remain centered and observe from there. Trust in yourself and your journey. If you have a gift, like intuition, don't let anyone dismiss it as mere superstition or irrationality.

Remember, you possess abilities that others may not, just as they have strengths you might lack. There is no need to absorb their negativity. Keep your faith simple, hold it close, and let it be your quiet source of strength.

Each experience, every joy and sorrow, adds to our own story, a story that only we can tell.

To surrender to life is not to give up; it is to open up. It's allowing life to reveal itself to us, trusting in its wisdom even when we do not fully understand.

Like a river that flows without asking where it goes, or a tree that grows without needing to know why, we too can surrender to the natural flow of existence.

When we embrace life with openness and wonder, the universe will respond, winking back at us, offering its wisdom in moments of quiet grace and sudden inspiration.

This surrender is not passive; it is a fearless embrace of the unknown. Just as the night trusts the dawn to bring light, so we can trust that life holds what we need. In that surrender, we find strength and a deep connection to the intelligence of all things.

## Embracing Interconnectedness

In many spiritual teachings, particularly Advaita Vedanta, there is a beautiful principle called **non-duality**. Non-duality means that everything—every person, creature, and particle of existence—is part of a unified whole.

At its core, this teaching suggests that all separation we perceive is an illusion. Imagine waves on an ocean: each wave appears distinct, rising and falling on its own, yet each is fundamentally one with the water.

Similarly, we see ourselves as separate individuals, yet we are like those waves on the vast ocean of existence, intrinsically connected to everything around us.

Recognizing this interconnectedness can change the way we experience life. When we understand that we are not isolated but part of a greater whole, we begin to see ourselves in others.

This insight allows us to transcend the boundaries of the ego—that part of us that often feels alone and separate—and embrace a wider identity that includes all of life.

We see others as mirrors, reflecting aspects of ourselves, and this understanding naturally fosters empathy and compassion. When we hurt another, we hurt ourselves; when we uplift another, we uplift the world.

In this state of **unity consciousness**, individual and universal awareness merge. This is not just a lofty idea; it's an experience of deep peace and clarity, where we feel connected to a source that holds us all.

It's a feeling of being "at home" in the universe, beyond fear, beyond isolation, knowing that we are part of something timeless and infinite.

### Cultivating Presence in Nature

Nature is perhaps the most direct expression of this unity. When we spend time in the natural world, we feel closer to the pulse of life, the same force that beats in our own hearts. Each leaf, each drop of rain, each breeze carries the quiet wisdom of the universe.

To truly connect with nature, we must slow down and become present, observing the intricate details around us—the patterns on a leaf, the sound of flowing water, the sensation of the wind on our skin.

This presence deepens our awareness, allowing us to feel life's intelligence and beauty more vividly.

Practices like walking barefoot on the earth can help ground us, connecting us physically and energetically to the planet. This grounding brings a sense of calm and balance, reminding us of our role within the larger ecosystem.

When we experience this connection, caring for the earth becomes natural; we see that by nurturing nature, we are also nurturing ourselves.

**Listening to the Universe**

To build a relationship with the universe, we must create space for open, silent communication. When we are quiet, the universe speaks—not in words but in a language of intuition and insight.

Meditation and periods of stillness allow us to hear this subtle guidance. In those moments, we may receive insights or inspirations that seem to come from nowhere but resonate deeply.

Trusting and following these intuitive nudges helps us align with the universe's flow, where life becomes less about struggle and more about ease. As we listen, we often find ourselves guided toward what is right for us, even if we don't fully understand it at the time.

**Practicing Gratitude**

Another powerful way to connect with the universe is through gratitude. When we regularly express thanks for the moments, people, and experiences in our lives, we strengthen our bond with existence.

Gratitude is like a bridge that brings us closer to the universe; it's a way of saying, "I see the gifts you bring, and I cherish them."

By being grateful, we open ourselves to receive more, creating a cycle of positivity that enriches our lives and deepens our connection to all that is.

As we embrace interconnectedness, we move through life with a sense of unity, peace, and reverence. This relationship with the universe is a dance—a quiet, trusting partnership where we surrender to life's mysteries, confident that we are part of a larger harmony.

## Understanding Synchronicities

Sometimes, life presents us with moments so perfectly aligned that they feel charged with meaning, yet there seems to be no logical explanation for them.

These are known as **synchronicities**, a term coined by the psychologist Carl Jung to describe "meaningful coincidences" that are not linked by cause and effect.

Synchronicities often carry a deep sense of awe, as though the universe itself is responding to our thoughts, feelings, or needs.

Imagine you're thinking about an old friend, and just then, you receive a message from them. Or perhaps you've been wrestling with a decision, and a sign appears that seems to answer your question.

These events seem too perfect to be mere chance, as if life itself is communicating with us.

Synchronicities act as mirrors, reflecting our inner world through outer events, reminding us of the mysterious, interconnected nature of reality.

## Modern Society and the Disconnect from Our Source

Modern society often measures success in terms of productivity and achievements, conditioning us to pursue one goal after another in an endless cycle.

The daily routine, often structured around a 9-to-5 job, can become an exhausting loop that leaves many feeling disconnected and unfulfilled, as though life is just a series of tasks rather than a journey of purpose and joy.

We're told we need money to live, to survive, but we forget that this system of earning, spending, and striving is one we created ourselves.

While society pushes us to consume and compete, we are subtly cut off from the abundant energy of the natural world, a source that provides freely and unconditionally.

The earth has always provided enough for all, but the greed of a few and the unawareness of many have led us to a place where much of humanity is caught in a cycle of desire, stress, and dissatisfaction—a loop that some traditions call the **wheel of samsara**, an endless cycle of craving and suffering.

## Breaking Free

To break free from this cycle, we need to change how we approach work and life. Instead of seeing work as mere duty or grind, we can turn it into a **practice of devotion** and a pathway for personal growth.

When we bring presence, compassion, and a sense of play into our work, we transform it into something more meaningful. Every task, no matter how small, becomes an opportunity for learning, for mastery, and for bringing a sense of peace and joy into our daily lives.

In yoga and spiritual traditions, the concept of **samadhi** describes a state of total absorption where one becomes so immersed in an activity that the sense of self dissolves, and what remains is pure, effortless presence.

Imagine bringing this quality of focus and love to your work—no matter what that work may be. When we find satisfaction in the present, the need for external rewards lessens.

True satisfaction arises from being fully engaged, from bringing our heart and soul into what we do, turning every action into a sacred offering.

## Ask Questions

To reclaim a life of purpose, we must first ask the important questions:

"What truly brings me fulfillment?"

"What do I value beyond the paycheck and the title?"

By questioning our habits and motives, we take charge of our lives, aligning our actions with our true desires rather than with society's expectations.

Be compassionate with yourself in this process, as it takes time to undo old patterns and create a new path forward.

Extend this compassion to others as well. Most people are carrying the weight of society's demands and expectations; a small act of kindness or understanding can make a profound difference.

When we lift each other up, we create a ripple effect, inspiring others to see life from a deeper, more fulfilling perspective.

## Play Your Part with Awareness and Joy

If we approach life as play rather than as duty, it opens up possibilities for joy. Society may define roles for us, but we have the power to choose how we embody them.

Find your joy in the present moment, in your unique skills, and in the positive impact you can make. Embrace the work you do as part of your spiritual growth, as a place where you can learn, evolve, and spread love and kindness.

In the fabric of the universe lies a profound balance, one that the mind alone cannot fully comprehend. The energy you give is the energy you receive, and what you receive can be transmuted and returned in a new form.

For instance, when you encounter anger, you have the power to remain centered, breathe, and respond with the energy of understanding. Alternatively, you can mirror the anger and return it unchanged. The choice is yours, yet the universal law of balance remains unwavering.

Remember, silence is the key. Within stillness, there is movement; within non-action, there is profound action. Trust the universe to balance itself through you. Become the divine instrument, fine-tuning yourself so that you can perform in harmony with the greater cosmic flow.

In this way, you are both the musician and the instrument, playing the symphony of life with grace and purpose.

As Rumi beautifully wrote,

"Let the beauty of what you love be what you do."

In reclaiming this connection to our source, to the essence of who we are beyond the daily grind, we find that life is filled with more than enough meaning, beauty, and love.

By living consciously, by choosing to work with joy and presence, we step off the wheel of samsara and into a life of purpose, connection, and inner freedom.

## Embracing Synchronicities

Synchronicities serve as reminders of our connection to the universe, subtle nudges that encourage us to awaken to life beyond the ordinary. They often arrive when we are open, when our attention is not fixed solely on achieving or acquiring but on simply being.

These moments have a unique way of reminding us to ask ourselves:

"What am I here for?

What truly matters?"

They urge us to look beyond material needs, beyond what media or society tells us to want, and to find joy and contentment in our own experiences.

When synchronicities occur, they often evoke a feeling of wonder and astonishment, as if we've glimpsed something beyond the everyday.

The timing of these events can be uncanny, showing up just when we need them most, providing insight, comfort, or direction.

They reflect our inner desires and intentions back to us in ways that feel intimately personal and relevant.

In Advaita Vedanta, synchronicities are seen as reminders of the **non-dual nature of reality**. They hint at the interconnectedness of the inner and outer worlds, as if life itself were a play of **Lila**, the divine dance where the universe and individual consciousness are intertwined.

When we see life as a dance between our inner and outer realities, we become more attuned to these signs, recognizing them as expressions of the universe's intelligence.

**Living with Awareness**

To fully appreciate synchronicities, it's important to live consciously, with a clear sense of who we are and what we truly value. Ask yourself:

Do I pursue what genuinely brings me joy, or am I following the path society has laid out for me?

When we are clear about our desires, aware of our strengths, and grateful for what we already have, we begin to live with a sense of fulfillment that doesn't rely on material gains or validation.

Synchronicities remind us that life is not just about chasing success or fitting into the mold that society dictates. Instead, they call us back to our roots, to a life of connection, simplicity, and awareness.

The universe responds when we engage with it openly, when we are willing to see beyond appearances and recognize that life is a vast, living mystery, brimming with wisdom and possibility.

To live in this way is to cultivate an open heart, a mind that sees meaning in each moment, and a soul that winks back at the universe, knowing that we are all part of this cosmic dance.

The next time a synchronicity occurs, let it be a reminder to look deeper, to live more authentically, and to trust that life itself is guiding you, one meaningful step at a time.

## Attracting Synchronicities

To attract synchronicities, begin by aligning your intentions with the natural flow of the universe. This means not only knowing what you want but feeling connected to it, harmonizing your inner desires with the world around you.

When our inner world is in alignment, we create a resonance that invites meaningful, guiding coincidences into our lives.

Start by setting clear intentions. Be specific about what you want to manifest or understand, and let yourself feel the emotions associated with achieving it—joy, gratitude, and fulfillment. These emotions help anchor your intentions, making them feel real and close.

Awareness is essential. Stay present and open, allowing yourself to notice subtle signs and unexpected opportunities. Approach each moment with a sense of curiosity and openness, as life often delivers answers in ways we may not anticipate.

Trust the process, releasing attachment to exact outcomes or strict timelines. By having faith in the universe's wisdom, you open yourself to receive guidance in its own timing and form.

Taking inspired action is also key. Pay attention to your intuition, acting on hunches that feel aligned with your intentions.

Small, proactive steps create momentum and signal your commitment to your goals, making space for synchronicities to unfold naturally.

Maintaining a positive state of mind and a high vibration also draws synchronicities. When you cultivate feelings of love, gratitude, and joy, you align yourself with the frequency of the universe.

Practices like yoga, tai chi, or energy work can support this, helping to balance and elevate your energy, making you more receptive to the flow of life.

Gratitude strengthens this connection. When synchronicities occur, acknowledge them with appreciation—this reinforces the bond between you and the universe.

Regular gratitude journaling can amplify this effect, lifting your energy and keeping you aligned with the abundance already present in your life.

Interestingly, concepts from quantum physics echo this idea of interconnectedness. Quantum entanglement suggests that particles are linked over vast distances, hinting at a deeper unity in the fabric of reality.

The observer effect shows that simply observing can influence outcomes, suggesting that our consciousness may play a role in shaping reality itself.

Though complex, these ideas support the notion that our intentions and awareness are part of a universal web of connection.

Incorporate synchronicities into your life by reflecting on their significance. Take time to understand the meaning behind these moments and how they relate to your path.

When we live in tune with the universe's flow, synchronicities become a natural part of our lives. Each one serves as a gentle nudge, guiding us toward greater awareness, wisdom, and personal transformation.

Living with this openness enriches our journey, connecting us to a larger rhythm where every moment holds potential for profound insight and growth.

## Differentiating Between Ego and Intuition

Understanding the difference between ego and intuition is essential for making choices that reflect our true selves. While the ego often speaks from a place of fear, control, and attachment, intuition arises from a calm, grounded knowing that aligns with our deeper values.

When we act from ego, our decisions are usually driven by insecurity, a need for external validation, or comparison with others. There's often a strong attachment to specific outcomes, a desire for recognition, and an underlying critical voice pushing us to act.

The ego may respond defensively or reactively, quick to shield itself from perceived threats, which can lead to actions that feel pressured or forced.

In contrast, intuitive guidance feels peaceful and clear, free from urgency or a need for personal gain. Intuition is detached from ego; it doesn't seek validation or focus on how actions will appear to others.

Instead, intuitive decisions resonate with our inner values and take into account the well-being of everyone involved.

Intuition often comes as gentle, persistent nudges that consistently steer our attention in a particular direction, encouraging us to act from authenticity rather than ambition.

For instance, an ego-driven decision might involve accepting a job purely for prestige or to compete with others, even if it doesn't align with our interests.

In contrast, an intuitive decision would mean choosing a career path that feels meaningful and fulfilling, even if it doesn't offer the highest status or income.

To distinguish between the two, ask yourself:

Am I driven by fear or love?

Am I attached to a specific outcome or genuinely aligned with my values?

Does this decision feel calm and grounded, or tense and pressured?"

Reflecting on these questions regularly can help strengthen your connection to intuition, allowing you to make choices that honor your true self over the ego's demands.

The idea is not to shun material gains, for spirituality and the material world are deeply interconnected. The point is to engage consciously, understanding your true values and where your attention—the real currency—flows.

Reflect for a moment on why nurses, who heal and support lives, are paid less than entertainers who provide temporary distraction. Or why school teachers, who shape the minds of the future, are often less respected than rappers.

These disparities reveal where society's collective intention lies and what our priorities truly are.

Now, reflect on this: if a nurse or a teacher were to win the lottery and suddenly become wealthy overnight, would they continue their work? This question probes deeper than it seems, revealing life's true complexity.

The reality is that no matter what you achieve or gain, if it is not aligned with your soul's path and your deepest inner values, it will bring no lasting peace. Material wealth or external success, though alluring, cannot fill the void left by a life lived out of sync with your true self.

The fulfillment comes from knowing that what you do resonates with your core, that your efforts serve both your spirit and the greater good.

Life's journey is not about collecting accolades or possessions, but about aligning each choice with the call of your soul. Without this alignment, all gains become hollow echoes of what you truly seek.

That is why the mystic truth resonates so profoundly:

You are exactly where you are supposed to be.

Every moment, every experience—whether filled with joy or challenge—is part of your unique path. Be present, and let bliss arise from this acceptance. This is your place, your moment.

Let go of guilt for past choices, fear of the unknown, and the cynicism that clouds the heart.

Embrace the now, for within it lies your true self, free and aligned with the essence of life. Trust this truth, and let it guide you toward peace and fulfillment.

Also remember to be wise, as Franz Kafka so poignantly warned:

"I was ashamed of myself when I realized that life was a costume party, and I attended with my real face."

Understand that beneath the masks we wear and the roles we play, there lies a deeper truth. Life invites us to look beyond appearances, to see the reality hidden behind the facade.

Wisdom comes in recognizing this, embracing the roles without becoming lost in them, and staying true to the essence of who you are beneath it all.

The spiritual journey requires this awareness. Know that life is a game, a grand stage where roles are played and masks are worn.

A spiritual seeker must not be naive, for naivety leaves one vulnerable to the shifting tides of external values.

Instead, be vigilant, observing with an inner knowing. Engage with life fully, but do so with discernment and wisdom.

Let your decisions come from a conscious place that honors both your material needs and your deeper, spiritual truths.

# Chapter 6:

# The Quantum Perspective

Quantum physics, the study of matter and energy at the smallest scales, has reshaped how we understand the universe.

It reveals a world far more interconnected and mysterious than we might imagine, offering insights that resonate deeply with our own experiences of consciousness and personal growth.

Exploring these principles can help us understand our connection to everything around us, inspiring us to live with greater awareness and openness.

## Quantum Principles and Personal Growth

Quantum physics introduces concepts that seem strange at first but hold powerful messages for how we experience life and growth.

### Wave-Particle Duality

In quantum physics, particles like electrons can act both as particles and waves, depending on how they are observed.

This duality reminds us of the dual nature of our own existence; we are both physical beings and beings of consciousness.

Embracing this duality allows us to see ourselves more holistically, recognizing our body, mind, and spirit as interconnected aspects of our being.

### The Uncertainty Principle

Proposed by Werner Heisenberg, this principle states that certain properties (like an electron's position and speed) cannot be known precisely at the same time. This fundamental uncertainty is a natural part of life.

It teaches us that not everything can be controlled or predicted, and by accepting this, we open ourselves to possibilities and reduce our anxieties. Embracing life's uncertainties can help us adapt, grow, and find peace within the unknown.

## Quantum Entanglement

When particles become entangled, their states remain connected, even across vast distances—changing one instantly affects the other.

This phenomenon suggests a profound unity, as if the universe itself is a web of interconnected relationships. Recognizing this unity invites us to foster empathy and a sense of belonging. As physicist Nikola Tesla once said,

"If you want to find the secrets of the universe, think in terms of energy, frequency, and vibration."

## Superposition

Quantum particles can exist in multiple states simultaneously until they are observed. This idea reflects the potential within each of us; until we make a choice, many possibilities are open to us.

Understanding our own potential reminds us that we are not limited by past experiences or labels; rather, each moment holds numerous paths, waiting for us to choose.

## The Observer Effect

In quantum physics, the act of observation affects the outcome of an experiment.

This suggests that our awareness and intentions play a role in shaping our reality. Our thoughts, attitudes, and beliefs influence how we experience the world.

When we are mindful of our thoughts, we bring greater intention to our lives and can shape our experiences in a more positive direction.

# Connecting Quantum Physics and Spirituality

The principles of quantum physics bear striking similarities to spiritual teachings, particularly those of non-duality, which is central to traditions like Advaita Vedanta. Non-duality, or the belief that all is one, tells us that separation is an illusion.

This mirrors quantum entanglement, which shows that everything is interconnected. Just as spiritual teachings urge us to see ourselves as part of a greater whole, quantum physics suggests that we are all connected on an energetic level.

Similarly, the illusion of separateness in spirituality aligns with the relational nature of particles in quantum physics; particles aren't isolated but are defined by their relationships.

Spiritual teachings often explain that the ego creates the illusion of separateness, while our true self is part of a universal whole. In both perspectives, understanding the unity behind apparent differences leads to a deeper peace and sense of connection.

The role of the observer in quantum physics resonates with the importance of consciousness in spirituality. Many spiritual traditions teach that our awareness shapes our reality, a concept reflected in the observer effect in physics.

Both science and spirituality reveal that our awareness has the power to transform our experience of the world.

Finally, superposition and potentiality in quantum physics suggest that multiple possibilities exist until a choice is made.

This aligns with the idea in spirituality that we are full of potential and that life offers countless paths, each unfolding according to our intentions and actions.

# Applying Quantum Ideas to Daily Life

Understanding these quantum principles allows us to approach life with a fresh perspective, where mystery and possibility are constants, inviting us to embrace a deeper relationship with ourselves and the world.

### Accept Uncertainty

Let go of the need to control every outcome. By accepting uncertainty, we create space for new possibilities and reduce stress. Embrace life with curiosity, and see what unfolds when you are open to the unknown.

### Harness Your Potential

Recognize that life holds multiple possibilities at every moment. Visualize your goals, set clear intentions, and take small steps toward what you want. By being proactive and open, you empower yourself to shape the life you desire.

### Be Mindful of Your Thoughts and Intentions

Recognize that your thoughts and attitudes influence your reality. Practice mindfulness and observe how your focus shapes your experiences, helping you live with greater purpose and awareness.

### Cultivate Connection

Acknowledge your connection to others and the environment. Engage in practices that foster empathy and compassion, whether through community involvement, environmental stewardship, or simply treating others with kindness.

### Embrace Both Rational and Intuitive Thinking

Honor the balance between logic and intuition, between physical reality and the unseen. This balance creates a more integrated and authentic self, allowing you to navigate life with wisdom and insight.

**Trust the Process**

Life's outcomes are not always predictable, and this is a part of the journey. Trusting in life's unfolding allows you to build resilience and approach challenges with a growth mindset, focusing on learning and personal evolution rather than simply on results.

When we combine quantum insights with non-dual philosophy, we can see ourselves as part of a unified whole. This shift in perspective helps us recognize that our limitations are often self-imposed.

By aligning ourselves with universal consciousness, we live in harmony with all that is, empowering us to manifest our intentions and consciously shape our lives.

In opening ourselves to the quantum perspective, we step into a space where science and spirituality meet, illuminating the nature of reality and our place within it.

This holistic understanding encourages us to live with greater awareness, intention, and openness to the infinite possibilities that life holds.

By embracing both the known and the mysterious, we live as both students and creators of our own experiences, discovering that life, in its essence, is both profoundly connected and infinitely expansive.

"You have the right to work, but for the work's sake only. You have no right to the fruits of work. Desire for the fruits of work must never be your motive in working. Never give way to laziness, either.

Perform every action with you heart fixed on the Supreme Lord. Renounce attachment to the fruits. Be even-tempered in success and failure: for it is this evenness of temper which is meant by yoga.

Work done with anxiety about results is far inferior to work done without such anxiety, in the calm of self-surrender. Seek refuge in the knowledge of Brahma. They who work selfishly for results are miserable."

— Bhagavad Gita

# Conclusion

In the silent chambers of the human heart lies a profound yearning—a whisper that speaks of the infinite, the eternal, the ineffable.

This guide has journeyed through the landscapes of self-love, fearlessness, and unity with the universe, weaving together the threads of psychology, philosophy, and mysticism.

Yet, as we stand at the edge of understanding, we confront the most profound aspects of existence: the deep sadness that sometimes envelops us, the void that echoes within, the undeniable reality of death, and the vast unknown that stretches beyond our comprehension.

## Embracing the Deep Sadness and the Void

Life, in all its beauty and complexity, is intertwined with moments of melancholy and emptiness. This deep sadness is not a sign of weakness but a testament to our capacity to feel deeply, to love profoundly, and to yearn for meaning in a world that often defies understanding.

The void we sense is a sacred space—a reminder of the infinite possibilities that reside within nothingness. It is in acknowledging this void that we open ourselves to transformation, allowing the old to fade and making room for new growth.

> "When meditation is mastered,
> The mind is unwavering like the
> Flame of a lamp in a windless place.
> In the still mind,
> In the depths of meditation,
> The Self reveals itself.
> Beholding the Self
> By means of the Self,
> An aspirant knows the
> Joy and peace of complete fulfillment.
> Having attained that
> Abiding joy beyond the senses,

> Revealed in the stilled mind,
> He never swerves from the eternal truth."
>
> — Bhagavad Gita

## The Reality of Death and the Unknown

Death stands as the ultimate mystery—the final chapter of our physical existence and the gateway to the unknown. It humbles us, reminding us of the transient nature of life and the preciousness of each moment.

Yet, within this inevitability lies a profound lesson: to live fully, to love without restraint, and to pursue our deepest truths. Embracing the reality of death encourages us to shed trivial pursuits and focus on what truly matters.

The unknown is not a void to be feared but a frontier to be explored. It is the canvas upon which we paint our destinies, the uncharted waters where potential becomes reality.

By stepping into the unknown with courage and openness, we honor the adventurous spirit that resides within each of us.

> "Death is as sure for that which is born, as birth is for that which is dead. Therefore grieve not for what is inevitable."
>
> — Bhagavad Gita

## Nothingness, God, and the Beyond

The concept of nothingness is a paradox—both the absence of all and the presence of infinite potential. In many spiritual traditions, it is within this nothingness that the divine is found.

God, the ultimate mystery, the source of all that is and is not, resides beyond the grasp of intellect yet is intimately known through the heart.

The beyond is not a distant realm but a dimension that interweaves with our reality. It whispers through the rustling leaves, glimmers in the stars, and resonates in the silence between our thoughts.

By attuning ourselves to this subtle realm, we tap into a wellspring of wisdom, love, and creativity that transcends the limitations of the ego.

## The Named is the Mother

> The Tao that can be told is not the eternal Tao.
> The name that can be named is not the eternal name.
> The nameless is the beginning of heaven and earth.
> The named is the mother of the ten thousand things.
> Ever desireless, one can see the mystery.
> Ever desiring, one can see the manifestations.
> These two spring from the same source but differ in name;
> this appears as darkness.
> Darkness within darkness.
> The gate to all mystery.
>
> — Tao Te Ching

In Taoist philosophy, the phrase "The named is the mother of ten thousand things" from the *Tao Te Ching* holds profound meaning and encapsulates the essence of manifestation and creation.

This line not only hints at the process by which the formless Tao gives rise to the tangible world but also symbolizes the role of feminine energy in the act of creation.

### The Unnamed and the Named

To fully understand the significance of "The named is the mother of ten thousand things," it is essential to grasp the dual aspects of the Tao as both the unnamable and the named.

The unnamable Tao represents the ultimate reality—the eternal, formless, and indefinable source of all that exists. It is beyond language, beyond comprehension, and cannot be captured by words or thoughts.

This is the essence of the Tao in its purest state: the origin of all existence and non-existence.

However, once the Tao takes form and is named, it transitions from the realm of the formless into the manifest world.

The act of naming signifies the beginning of creation, where the Tao becomes knowable and enters the realm of duality. This duality, inherent in all aspects of existence, is symbolized by the concepts of *yin* and *yang*.

**Feminine Energy as the Creative Force**

The phrase "The named is the mother of ten thousand things" embodies the principle of *yin*, the feminine energy that represents receptivity, nurturing, and creation.

In Taoist cosmology, *yin* is the counterpart to *yang* (masculine energy), and together they form the balance of all existence.

While *yang* is associated with activity, assertion, and illumination, *yin* embodies the qualities of stillness, receptivity, and the potential for creation.

In many spiritual and philosophical traditions, the feminine energy is seen as the womb of creation—the space in which potential becomes form.

This idea aligns with the concept that the "named" Tao acts as the "mother," bringing forth the multiplicity of the universe.

Just as a mother nurtures life within her, the feminine principle in Taoism is the source from which the "ten thousand things" (a metaphor for the innumerable forms of existence) emerge.

## Transition from Formless to Form

When the Tao is unnamed, it represents the boundless, undivided source of all. The moment it is named—when it becomes known or understood—it shifts into the realm of manifestation.

This process can be seen as the point where the undivided Tao expresses itself in the form of creation, moving from potential to actuality.

This shift is inherently feminine because it mirrors the generative power attributed to *yin*. The act of giving birth, nurturing growth, and creating life is symbolically connected to the "mother" archetype.

The named Tao, therefore, becomes the "mother" that births all forms, embodying the nurturing energy that sustains and supports life.

This highlights the profound idea that the source of all manifested existence is rooted in the feminine aspect of the Tao.

## Ten Thousand Things

In the *Tao Te Ching*, "ten thousand things" is a traditional phrase that signifies the multiplicity of all creation—the entire spectrum of existence.

The line "The named is the mother of ten thousand things" implies that once the Tao moves from being unmanifest (unnamed) to manifest (named), it becomes the origin of everything in the universe.

The feminine, *yin* energy, therefore, is the bridge between the formless and the formed, guiding the Tao's expression into the material world.

## Desire and Perception

"Ever desireless, one can see the mystery. Ever desiring, one can see the manifestations."

This reflects the way human perception is influenced by desire. When one is free from desire, they can perceive the true, underlying mystery of the Tao—the unnamable source.

However, when caught in desire, they only see the manifestations—the named and differentiated aspects of existence.

One can experience both the unmanifested and the manifested aspects of existence by engaging in different practices.

Through deep meditation, one accesses the unmanifested—the pure, formless essence of the Tao where the mystery is realized beyond thought and desire. This is where one encounters the profound stillness and unity of all things.

On the other hand, the manifested world can be experienced through the Law of Decree, where focused intention and spoken affirmation bring desires into reality.

This practice aligns one's energy with the creative force of the universe, making the intangible tangible and allowing the manifestations of one's will to take form.

In this way, both the mystery and the manifestations coexist as two expressions of the same source.

## Darkness Within Darkness

"Darkness within darkness. The gateway to all understanding," symbolizes the profound mystery of the Tao.

The term "darkness" in Taoism often represents the unfathomable depth of the source, where all creation begins. It is within this darkness that the feminine energy—the mother of all—resides, holding the potential for all manifestations.

Understanding this part of the *Tao Te Ching* requires an appreciation of the role of *yin*, the feminine energy, as the foundation for creation.

The "named" Tao as the "mother" reflects the eternal principle that in the process of naming and manifesting, the nurturing force of the feminine is ever-present, shaping and sustaining the universe.

"The named is the mother of ten thousand things" encapsulates the Taoist view of manifestation through feminine energy.

When the Tao enters the realm of the named, it embodies the nurturing, creative force that gives rise to the world of form.

The feminine principle, with its qualities of receptivity, stillness, and creation, plays a crucial role in this process.

In understanding this, we gain insight into the profound balance of *yin* and *yang* and the ultimate mystery of existence—the gateway to all understanding.

## Faith and Hope as Guiding Stars

In the face of life's uncertainties and existential questions, faith and hope emerge as guiding stars.

Faith is not blind belief but a deep trust in the underlying goodness of existence and the inherent meaningfulness of our journey. It is the anchor that holds us steady amid life's tempests.

Hope kindles the light within us, illuminating the path forward even when the way seems obscured. It inspires us to envision a better future, to strive for growth, and to believe in the possibility of transformation—both within ourselves and in the world around us.

## The Journey Forward

As we conclude this exploration, we recognize that self-love and fearlessness are not destinations but ongoing practices—a dance with the rhythms of life. They invite us to embrace our humanity fully, with all its light and shadow, joy and sorrow.

By integrating the insights from psychology, Advaita Vedanta, and Taoism, we cultivate a deeper understanding of ourselves and our place in the cosmos.

We learn to navigate the delicate balance between embracing the present moment and yearning for the infinite, between honoring our individuality and recognizing our oneness with all that exists.

In this journey, we are not alone. The universe moves with us, responding to our intentions, reflecting our inner states, and offering guidance through synchronicities and intuitive whispers.

By attuning ourselves to this cosmic dialogue, we become co-creators of our reality, shaping our lives with purpose and passion.

In life, there are moments when we find ourselves staring into a profound existential void, a vast emptiness that echoes within. These experiences can feel overwhelming, urging us to turn away or seek distraction.

But in these moments, resist the temptation to flee. Sit with the feeling, letting yourself experience it fully. As Friedrich Nietzsche wisely observed,

> "He who fights with monsters should look to it that he himself does not become a monster."

When we face our own inner abyss with courage, we guard against losing ourselves to fear or bitterness; instead, we emerge with a greater strength.

Nietzsche also reminds us,

> "And if you gaze long enough into an abyss, the abyss will gaze back into you."

When we bravely hold our gaze within, exploring this inner depth, something extraordinary begins to happen. In the stillness of that encounter, beyond our fears and defenses, we discover that the emptiness is not a void to be feared but a space holding limitless potential.

The Upanishads echo this wisdom, teaching us that

> "Tat Tvam Asi"—"You are That."

We are not separate from the boundless source of existence but are made of it. The abyss within is a reflection of the vastness beyond, an opening to our own wholeness.

By embracing this depth, by allowing ourselves to descend fully into the core of our own being, a quiet yet powerful realization emerges: **we are enough**. As the Brihadaranyaka Upanishad teaches,

> "You are your own refuge; there is no other refuge."

From this inner refuge, we understand that our completeness has always been within us. This wholeness is not a fleeting feeling but a profound knowing that within us lies everything we need.

From this realization flows true compassion and love, both for ourselves and for others. It is a love born not of dependency or need but of a pure recognition of our shared essence.

This is the love that connects us effortlessly to all of life, a love that transcends fear, binds us to our deepest self, and brings a sense of peace that is both boundless and unshakeable.

Embracing this truth, we find that we are indeed one with All, capable of living with a heart full of compassion and a soul at rest in the vastness of existence.

The Void is the infinite source, boundless energy itself. Sit within it, alone, eyes closed, and attune to a single vibrational hum. When this sound has dissolved, release even that, entering the stillness beyond thought.

In that emptiness, let yourself be renewed. Emerge, and let this energy flow outward for the good of all. It is easier to drop one thought than to let go of thousands.

When you focus on one vibrational sound and release it, you reach Turiya, the Fourth state, beyond the trinity of waking, dreaming, and deep sleep.

Be mindful of what you decree to the universe under the Law of Decree in the Fourth state! The best decree is **silence**.

# Afterword

As you step away from these pages, remember that true spirituality is not a journey of naivety but one of conscious awareness and discernment. Not everyone deserves your help, and not every situation calls for your compassion.

This doesn't mean abandoning your dharma or your responsibilities; it means approaching them with wisdom rather than with guilt or fear.

It's about discerning when to engage and when to step back, understanding that true compassion includes setting boundaries and acting from a place of inner strength.

In this way, you honor both yourself and the greater purpose you serve, ensuring that your actions are rooted in clarity and balance.

In the end, love always wins—that is the universal law. It is the force that transcends all boundaries, heals all wounds, and unites everything in its path.

No matter the challenges or darkness encountered, love remains the ultimate truth, guiding us back to our true essence and illuminating the path forward.

Approach others with clarity; understand that some people act unconsciously, projecting shadows they are unaware of onto others.

It is essential to prioritize yourself first—to cultivate self-love and strength within. Only from a well-nourished, centered self can love and compassion truly expand outward.

As Lao Tzu once said,

> "When you are content to be simply yourself and don't compare or compete, everyone will respect you."

Make this wisdom a guiding principle in your life. Being compassionate doesn't mean tolerating abuse or crossing your own boundaries. Strengthen your boundaries, making them firm yet loving, so that they protect you without isolating you.

Recognize that your kindness does not require you to sacrifice your well-being. True spiritual growth calls for courage, even if that means taking tough decisions or walking away from situations that drain you.

In this world, each of us has personal lessons to learn, often through hardship. The universe does not show favoritism, nor does it alter its natural laws for any individual. We each walk our own path, learning and growing through our unique experiences.

Spirituality does not mean being a passive recipient of life's circumstances; it means approaching life with wisdom, strength, and a commitment to growth.

There is a balance between compassion for others and self-respect, and the journey of spirituality requires us to respect both.

Self-care is your foundation—build it wisely. Exercise, nourish your body with healthy food, and ground yourself through practices like breathwork, which becomes your anchor. Over time, you will feel your inner energy rise, strengthening your mind, body, and spirit.

See people as they are, without projecting your ideals or naivety onto them.

When you maintain clear boundaries, you create a sacred space that only the truest parts of yourself and the universe can enter. Within this boundary lies your own Self, the infinite void and potential, your source of strength.

Take time to sit with yourself, embracing moments of solitude. Don't run from these spaces of silence; they are where real insights emerge.

Always remember, **silence is the key**. Here are two quotes from Lao Tzu that will help you on this journey.

"Silence is a source of great strength."

"He who knows, does not speak. He who speaks, does not know."

### Embrace Playfulness in Transformation

Growth need not be a solemn path. Allow humor and lightness to accompany your journey. A playful approach eases the tension, breaking free from rigid expectations and making inner work feel more like discovery than discipline.

Transformation, as it unfolds, brings both light and shadow; embracing this duality invites us to see complexity as a source of richness. When we balance the serious with the lighthearted, growth becomes joyful.

### Acknowledge Life's Lessons

Reflect on the experiences that brought you here. Express gratitude for each lesson—good or bad—for they shape your path. As the journey continues, let gratitude be your anchor.

The "thank you" you offer to each moment brings peace, grounding you in an appreciation of the journey as it unfolds.

### Balance Complexity and Simplicity

Life is full of intricate patterns, yet simplicity lies at its core. Find a balance between understanding life's depth and enjoying its simple moments.

Just as the intricate swirls around a smile suggest both complexity and ease, remember to look deeply without losing the joy of simply being. This balance brings a sense of acceptance and peace.

## Commit to Self-Exploration

Self-exploration is not a destination but an ongoing practice. Set aside time to deepen your journey within, approaching your inner world with curiosity and openness.

Transformation is a steady commitment, one that unfolds step-by-step, bringing clarity, strength, and a deeper connection with yourself.

This journey reflects a blend of playfulness, complexity, self-expression, and transformation. As you embrace both your shadow and your light, remember that true growth requires joy as much as introspection.

Approach yourself with openness and a willingness to explore the unknown within. Life's lessons, though sometimes challenging, are here to enrich and shape you.

Find the balance between introspection and joy, and remember that transformation is both serious and light, inviting you to grow with both intention and ease.

> "Know thyself, and thou shall know all the mysteries of the gods and of the universe."

# Affirmations

# Inspired by Advaita Vedanta

- I am one with the infinite source of all existence.
- I am complete; within me lies all that I need.
- I am not this body, nor this mind; I am pure awareness.
- I am the witness of my thoughts, separate from them.
- I am eternal, beyond birth and death.
- I am the silent presence that remains, untouched by change.
- I am whole and perfect as I am.
- I am the space in which all experiences arise and dissolve.
- I am peace itself, beyond the pull of desires.
- I am boundless and free, unconfined by any form.
- I am rooted in the truth that transcends the seen and unseen.
- I am love in its purest form, flowing from within.
- I am free from attachment; nothing can diminish me.
- I am in all things, and all things are in me.
- I am light, illuminating all that I perceive.
- I am the stillness beneath the movement of life.
- I am here, now, embracing the essence of presence.
- I am the eternal Self, beyond the illusions of the world.
- I am the fullness within the emptiness.
- I am untouched by fear, as my essence is unchanging.
- I am that I am, the formless and the infinite.

# Embracing the Abyss

# A Poem

In the silent heart, a yearning speaks—
Of endless stars and mountain peaks.
A whisper lost in deep desire,
An ember of the soul's own fire.

Self-love, fearlessness—a path well-tread,
Through shadows deep and light ahead.
But at the edge, we pause and see,
The sadness vast, the void that breathes.

Don't turn away, don't flee the night;
Sit with the emptiness, hold it tight.
For wisdom warns with eyes so stern:
"Fight not with darkness lest you turn."

And if into the abyss you stare,
The depths will meet you, stark and bare.
Not as an enemy but a friend,
A depth that brings you home again.

Death, that mystery, cold and near,
Whispers, "Live fully, love without fear."
The unknown isn't dark or bleak,
But fertile ground for what we seek.

Nothingness holds infinite chance,
Where silence meets the cosmic dance.
The vast unknown, both far and near—
Felt in the heart, though never clear.

Faith and hope are stars at sea,
Guiding us through what's yet to be.
Not blind belief, but trust profound—
That in this journey, truth is found.

So here we are, not at an end,
But at a start where self extends.
We gaze within and find we're whole—
An ancient truth that stirs the soul.

A timeless voice might softly say,
"You are That"—you've found your way.
The abyss within reflects the sky;
You are enough; you need not try.

Compassion blooms from this embrace,
A love that transcends time and space.
So sit awhile, don't rush to move—
For in this stillness, love will prove.

That you and all the stars above,
Are bound together—bound by love.
In vastness deep, we rest and know,
We're one with All—above, below.

Printed in Great Britain
by Amazon